TEEN GUIDE TO STAYING SOBER

There are many forms of help available for teens who become addicted to alcohol. You are not alone.

HAZELDEN/ROSEN DRUG ABUSE PREVENTION LIBRARY

TEEN GUIDE TO STAYING SOBER

Christina Chiu

A HAZELDEN/ROSEN Book

Published in 1998 by The Rosen Publishing Group, Inc.
29 East 21st Street, New York, NY 10010

Copyright © 1998 by The Rosen Publishing Group, Inc.

This edition published in 1998 by Hazelden
P.O. Box 176, Center City, MN 55012-0176

First Edition

Library of Congress Cataloging-in-Publication Data

Chiu, Christina
    Teen guide to staying sober / Christina Chiu — 1st ed.
    p. cm. — (The drug abuse prevention library)
    Includes bibliographical references (p. 62) and index.
    Summary: Discusses the social and physical effects of alcohol, the reasons teenagers drink, the problems caused by teenage alcoholism, and possible preventive measures and treatments.
    ISBN 1-56838-249-9
    1. Alcoholism—United States—Prevention—Juvenile literature. 2. Teenagers—Alcohol use—United States—Juvenile literature. 3. Alcohol—Physiological effect—Juvenile literature. 4. Alcoholics—Rehabilitation—Juvenile literature. [1. Alcoholism.] I. Title. II. Series.
    HV5066.C484 1998
    362.292'7'08350973—dc21   98-16213
                                                                  CIP
                                                                  AC

Manufactured in the United States of America

Contents

Introduction

It's a typical Friday night. Sarah and her friends are heading over to Jason's to hang out for a while. When they get to Jason's house, they notice everyone is drinking beer. Some people are beginning to get totally wasted. Sarah doesn't want to drink tonight, but she doesn't want to look like a loser in front of everyone.

"Well, maybe just a couple of beers," Sarah tells herself. "Two beers can't hurt."

You know the deal. It seems like everyone else is drinking. Your friends pour you a drink. You want to say no—you know you have to drive later, or maybe you just don't feel like drinking. But everyone is watching, and you want to fit in and not seem like a loser.

So, like Sarah, maybe you take a drink. It gives you a buzz. Your friends give you another beer, so you drink that too. Before you know it, you're drunk. Soon you may find yourself caught in a pattern of partying and drinking every week.

It's almost two o'clock. Math class is just about over. John glances at the clock again. He's thinking about the bottle of rum hidden in the back of his closet. "I need a drink," he thinks. He can't wait. Nothing matters more to him right now than having a drink.

John knows he shouldn't drink so much. He tells himself he doesn't need it. He could stop if he wanted to, but not today. Maybe tomorrow.

If you find yourself in a situation like John's, you are not alone. The U.S. Department of Health and Human Services reports that one in every eight twelve-year-olds is a binge drinker. That means he or she consumes five or more alcoholic drinks in a row, and in most cases, he or she isn't aware that alcohol is a serious drug that can kill. Like John, many teens are addicted to alcohol. They want to get sober. The question is, how? This book will help teens learn how to overcome alcohol abuse and stay sober.

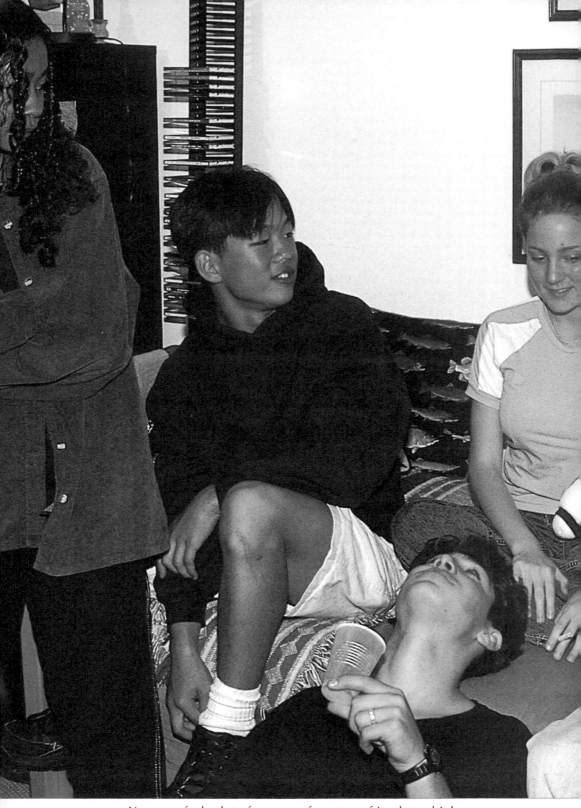

You may feel a lot of pressure from your friends to drink.

CHAPTER 1

Alcohol: An Overview

Bob wakes up at noon on a Saturday. For a moment, he doesn't know where he is. He looks around and realizes he's in his own room. Bob remembers hanging out at his friend's house playing a drinking game last night. He vaguely remembers that Diana, his ex-girlfriend, showed up at the party. She was with her new boyfriend. Bob can't remember if anything happened. Did he say anything to her? Bob can't even remember how he got home.

Bob can smell fried eggs and bacon cooking in the kitchen. He wants a drink of water, but the smell of breakfast makes his stomach turn. Bob pulls a pillow over his throbbing head. It feels as if there were a vise clamped around his temples. He turns over and tries to go back to sleep.

10 | *Your Brain on Alcohol*

Your brain is like a message center that controls everything in your body. Because alcohol is a depressant, it slows down messages that the brain sends or receives. This results in slowed or impaired vision, hearing, and coordination. That's why people under the influence of alcohol often slur their words or have difficulty walking. That's also why you should avoid driving when you've been drinking.

Alcohol also impairs your judgment and your ability to concentrate. You may take more risks such as picking a fight or having unprotected sex, which could lead to an unplanned pregnancy or a sexually trans- mitted disease (STD). Your emotions may run high, making you feel really happy, friendly, sad, or even angry. You may even black out and not remember what hap- pened while you were drinking.

Long-term use of alcohol can cause a loss of brain tissue. This loss can forever change your ability to think abstractly, solve problems, and remember things.

Your Body on Alcohol

Besides damaging your brain, alcohol can severely damage other body organs. The organ that is most affected by alcohol is

It is important not to mix drinking and driving because alcohol impairs your judgment and slows down your reaction time.

your liver. People who drink excessively for many years often start to show signs of liver disease. The most serious liver condition is cirrhosis. This is when the liver becomes so damaged that it fails to function.

Long-term alcohol abuse also puts you at greater risk of developing cancer, heart disease, and digestive problems. It may lead to impotence and lower sperm counts in men and the inability to bear children in women.

It is especially important for a teen, whose body is experiencing a lot of growth and change, to steer clear of alcohol. Like other drugs, alcohol affects the natural chemical reactions in your body, which may stunt your growth process.

12 | ## *The Law*

In the United States, it is illegal to buy or possess alcohol if you are under the age of twenty-one. Anyone who sells alcohol to a minor is breaking the law. In fact, establishments that sell alcohol must check identification to verify that you are over twenty-one years of age. Parents who let their children serve alcohol at parties are breaking the law.

Drinking and Driving: Zero Tolerance

Laws regulating drinking and driving exist to protect you as well as others from getting injured or killed. In all states, it is illegal for anyone to drive when his or her blood alcohol concentration (BAC), or the amount of alcohol in a person's system, reaches a certain level. BAC limits are determined by each state.

Thirty-seven states have even adopted zero-tolerance laws. This means that it is illegal in these states for anyone under age twenty-one to drive after drinking any amount of alcohol.

These laws are in place to try to prevent alcohol-related deaths. You may not care about the laws and believe that you are careful enough. However, it is hard to ignore the fact that about half of all fatal automobile crashes involve alcohol.

CHAPTER 2

The Dangers of Addiction

What's the first thing that comes to mind when you think of an alcoholic? Someone who is drunk all day, every day? Someone who can't hold down a job or doesn't have any friends?

The truth is that alcoholism is a disease that can affect anyone, regardless of age, gender, or race. He could be your next door neighbor. She could be a friend at school.

Alcoholics have a psychological or physical addiction to alcohol. A person doesn't have to drink all the time to have a drinking problem. Many alcoholics can mask their problems for many years until their conditions become so severe they can't be ignored.

The scary thing about drinking is that no one ever thinks that he or she will

Drinking may help some people to feel better for a while, but not for long. Problems will resurface when the alcohol wears off.

become addicted. People usually start drinking socially with friends. When someone becomes addicted, the disease takes over before he or she even realizes what's going on.

Not everyone who has one drink is going to become an alcoholic. However, many recovering alcoholics say that they never would have taken that first drink if they knew it would be addictive for them.

Stages of Addiction
Addiction isn't about willpower—or a lack of it. Alcohol, like other drugs, can create a temporary high that becomes an escape from one's problems. Addiction

14

usually occurs in several stages. These include experimentation, reinforcement, dependency, and denial.

If an addict doesn't get a fix, he or she will start to experience withdrawal symptoms. If the person can't stop, because of either physical or emotional reasons, then he or she has an addiction. The following is an explanation of what happens to a person's body at each stage of addiction.

Experimentation
There are many reasons, such as poor self-esteem, curiosity, boredom, peer pressure, or stress, that lead people to start drinking too much. A person might enjoy the high and be able to escape temporarily whatever bad feelings he or she has.

Reinforcement
People might believe that alcohol helps them be less inhibited so that they fit in with peers better. Or they might think it helps them block out problems. At this stage, people might be convinced that the "harmless" buzz is worth repeating. After a while, however, the body builds up a tolerance to alcohol and requires more and more of the drug to get that same high. Some experts call this the warning stage.

16 | ## Dependency

The more someone drinks, the more he or she will need to drink in order to get a buzz. The drug becomes both an emotional and a physical crutch. If an alcoholic doesn't get enough alcohol, he or she will begin to suffer from withdrawal symptoms. This is sometimes referred to as the danger stage.

Denial

Denial occurs when someone is drinking more and more heavily but refuses to acknowledge it, even if a friend expresses concern. A person in denial might say things like, "Get off my back, I'm not a drunk" or "I could quit right now if I wanted to" or "I don't drink any more than anyone else does."

The reality is that you can drink less than other people and still be an alcoholic. You can even be a functional alcoholic, which means that you look and act fine to those around you, even though you are drunk or have a drinking problem.

Withdrawal Symptoms

After a period of alcohol abuse, the body becomes dependent on the drug. Taking it away or reducing the amount causes the body to react. When an alcoholic starts to tremble and shake, he or she is in withdrawal. Other

Alcoholism is a disease that can affect anyone, regardless of age, gender, race, or class.

18 | signs of withdrawal include anxiety, trouble concentrating, nausea, and headaches. These symptoms can get worse and lead to hallucinations and seizures.

During this stage, an alcoholic loses control of his or her drinking habit. Alcoholics get so drunk they black out, or drink so much that they forget what they've done during certain periods of time.

Addiction

Alcoholics can't stop drinking without suffering from withdrawal. They even start to crave alcohol, feeling they need it to survive. At this point, an alcoholic finds comfort in staying drunk and often stops making excuses for his or her drinking.

Binge Drinking

Many people who become alcoholics go through the stages of addiction, gradually increasing the quantity and frequency of their alcohol intake. They are sometimes called problem drinkers.

A type of problem drinker who is often overlooked is the person who parties hard during the weekends, bingeing on five or more drinks in a row. Also overlooked are individuals who drink a lot, but only a few times a year. Binge drinking can lead to blackouts, alcohol poisoning, and poor decision making, such as having unprotected sex or driving under the influence.

Children of Alcoholics

Eric is heading home from baseball tryouts. He's excited to be one of the few sophomores to make the varsity team. But as he nears his house, a queasy feeling comes over him. "What if Mom has been drinking again?" he wonders. "Will she be crying or throwing a tantrum?"

Eric finds his mother weeping in her bedroom, an empty bottle of wine tucked by her side. When he asks her what is wrong, she snaps, "Where were you? I was waiting for you all day."

Eric apologizes. He feels a little guilty, as if he has let her down. But he is also angry that she can't take care of herself. She continues to cry. "You're the only one who cares," she tells him. "I need you."

After several hours, his mother finally falls asleep. He tucks her into bed and leaves the room. He locks himself in his room and stares at the ceiling. He is too exhausted to deal with homework or dinner. After school the next day, he tells his coach he can't be on the team. When his coach questions him about it, he makes up an excuse.

If you have a parent or a close relative who suffers from alcoholism, you're at risk

Children of Alcoholics

- Experts say there are more than 28 million children of alcoholics in the United States.

- Nearly 7 million children of alcoholics are young children or teenagers. Three million of these young children of alcoholics will abuse alcohol or drugs at some point in their lives.

- Children of alcoholics are four times more likely to become alcoholics than children of nonalcoholics.

- The National Institute on Alcohol Abuse and Alcoholism reports that children of alcoholics are at risk for emotional, behavioral, and learning problems. But many of these children—59 percent—do not develop any problems.

of developing the disease, too. Studies show
that children of alcoholics may start drinking as early as their teen or preteen years.
Once they begin drinking, they go through
the stages of alcoholism very quickly.

Why a Higher Risk of Alcoholism?

The following are some reasons why children of alcoholics are considered to be at a
higher risk for becoming alcoholics.

One or both parents are alcoholics. Alcoholism
runs in families. This means there's a like-
lihood that a person will suffer from alcoholism if another family member is an
alcoholic. This does not mean that you will
definitely become an alcoholic. But to
avoid developing a dependency, children of
alcoholics should consider not drinking
alcohol at all.

Coping problems. Forty-one percent of
children of alcoholics develop serious
problems coping with their emotions. If
they start drinking, they might be tempted
to use alcohol to escape from dealing with
emotions or difficult situations.

Learned behavior patterns. Children of
alcoholics learn unhealthy living patterns

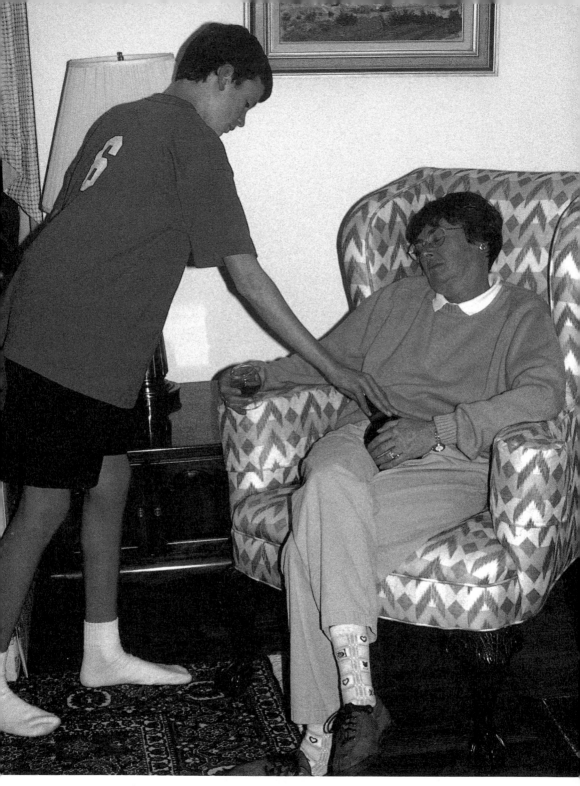

If you are the son or daughter of an alcoholic, you may consider joining a support group such as Alateen.

from their alcoholic parents. They tend to relate to other people the way their parents do. As a result, they lack the skills they need to deal with tough situations or to build good relationships. This may lead them to try to solve problems the way their parents do—through drinking.

How Are Children of Alcoholics Affected?

The alcoholic parent isn't the only one who suffers from the addiction. All family members, especially children, are affected by it. As a result of a parent's alcoholism, children tend to:

Adapt to chaos. Children of alcoholics typically live in homes that are in constant upheaval. In adapting to their unstable surroundings, they often develop low self-esteem, are depressed or feel isolated, and have difficulty maintaining healthy, long-term relationships. If these problems aren't resolved, they will continue through adult life.

Experience psychological problems. Children of alcoholics are more likely to have learning disabilities, suffer from anxiety and depression, and attempt suicide.

24 *Hide problems.* Children of alcoholics tend to be approval seekers. Many try to maintain peace and calm within their households and try to head off problems before they start. If they see something wrong, they try to fix it. They try to help everyone else at the expense of their own well-being. This kind of behavior may help others, but it hides problems.

How to Cope in an Alcoholic Family
In most families with an alcoholic parent, the family often doesn't cope with the problem. Facing up to the problem can seem like too much of a threat to the family. A nonalcoholic family member might also be in denial about the alcoholic's condition and may rescue the alcoholic by lying or covering up for him or her. This person is called an enabler.

Enablers think they are acting out of love or caring. In reality, they are helping the alcoholic's disease go untreated. Experts say the best way to help addicts is to let them suffer the consequences of their actions whenever possible. This doesn't mean that a person should let someone drive while drunk. It may mean not covering up or lying for the alcoholic anymore. It is hoped that this will force the

alcoholic to face his or her problem and
seek help.

Another way to help an alcoholic family member is to work with a trained professional to do an intervention. This occurs when family and friends of the dependent person confront him or her about the problem. They try to help the alcoholic realize that he or she needs help. Then they work together to get the dependent person into treatment right away.

If you arc the child of an alcoholic, you are not alone. There are people who can help. Alateen is an organization created specifically for teens like you. There are Alateen groups across the United States and the world. Members of the group learn to deal with their problems by supporting one another and sharing their experiences. Alateen helps young people understand their parents' problems and the disease of alcoholism.

Gold-medal Olympic figure skater Oksana Baiul is a recovering alcoholic.

CHAPTER 3

Teens and Alcohol

Tony tells himself he has to stop. No more drinking. Last week he got into a drunken brawl with a guy at a party. Yesterday he drank so much he passed out before school. If his mother hadn't left for work early that day, she would have found him on the bathroom floor. Right now, he can't stop thinking about the bottle of vodka that is hidden in the back of his dresser drawer. He believes that the only way he won't drink is if he gets out of the house.

But getting away doesn't help. On his way to his friend's house, he sees alcohol advertisements all over buses and telephone booths. The liquor store around the corner is advertising a sale on his favorite beer. Little by little, Tony feels his will giving way as his craving grows.

28

Tony is practically shaking by the time he reaches Hin Yu's house. A bunch of friends are watching a movie. Tony joins them and can smell the beer on Hin Yu's breath.

"Want a beer?" Hin Yu asks.

Tony thinks, "Don't do it." But by now, he's shaking so much that he tells himself, "Well, maybe just one."

Take a look around. Images that make drinking look cool are everywhere. You open a magazine, and the first thing you might find is a vodka advertisement. Some people wear beer slogans on their T-shirts. On television and in the movies, you see your favorite celebrities drinking certain brands of alcohol. Then, at the next party you go to, you notice that brand is what everyone is drinking. What you may not know is that beer and alcohol companies pay to have their products appear in a film or on television.

Glamorous and rebellious images often come with drinking. These ideas are supported by direct advertising, such as magazine ads, television commercials, and billboards. These images are also brought to you indirectly through movies and television shows. Movie and television producers use anything that will draw you

Alcohol-related car crashes are the number-one killer of teenagers in the United States.

to their shows, and they know that drugs, sex, and violence attract audiences. Why? Because many people, especially teens, think it's cool to be rebellious and reckless.

The Not-So-Glamorous Facts About Teens and Alcohol

Alcohol-related car crashes are the number-one killer of teens in the United States. The National Highway Traffic Safety Administration (NHTSA) reports that in 1996, there were 2,315 drivers age fifteen to twenty years old who died in alcohol-related car crashes.

According to the Center for Substance Abuse Prevention (CSAP), eight young people die every day in the United States

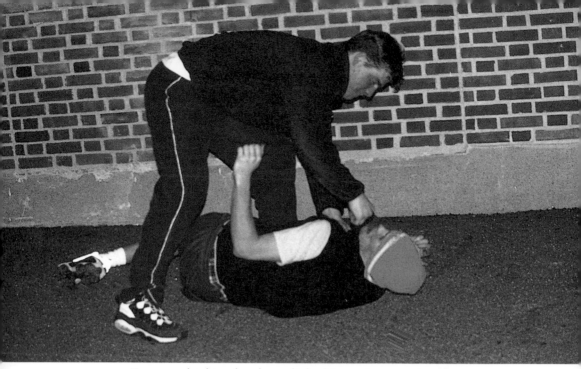

Teenage drinking has been linked to an increase in crime. Alcohol can cause aggression and violence, whether it's inside the home or out on the streets.

as a result of alcohol-related automobile crashes. Young people account for 7 percent of the nation's driving population, yet they are responsible for 12 percent of fatal crashes.

Car crashes aren't the only problems caused by excessive drinking. Alcohol also increases the risk of aggressive behavior, violence, and other risky behaviors. Teenage drinking has been linked to an increase in crime, stranger and date rape, victimization, pregnancy, use of illegal drugs such as cocaine and heroin, and teenage suicide. Here are some related national statistics.

Injury and Death

One teen dies in an alcohol-related car

crash every 3 hours. These crashes are the leading cause of injury and death in teens today.

Crime
Close to 40 percent of the young people serving a sentence in adult correctional facilities said they were drinking before they committed their crimes.

Victimization
More than 50 percent of crime victims were under the influence of alcohol at the time they were physically or sexually assaulted.

Pregnancy and STDs
Studies show that 95 percent of all teenage pregnancies occur when one or both part-ners are under the influence of drugs or alcohol. One study also shows that nearly one-third of college women diagnosed with a sexually transmitted disease (STD) were drunk at the time of infection.

Why Do Teens Drink?

Anxiety and Depression
Alcohol is a mind-altering drug that can change your mood. Some people use alco-hol as a crutch to calm themselves if they're

32 feeling anxious about something. Others drink to avoid the real issues that trouble them when they're feeling down. Drinking may help them feel better for a little while, but not for long. When people don't deal with the source of their problems, they often find their anxiety and depression become worse.

Abuse

Teens who are abused either emotionally, sexually, or physically by a parent, relative, friend, or stranger are at high risk of depression and other problems. They may feel they need to hide their secrets and are scared to get help from others.

Many teens who have been abused struggle with feelings of guilt and shame. They believe they have done something wrong to bring out such behavior from their abusers. Believing that there's no way out, many teens turn to drugs and alcohol to solve their emotional problems. For a few hours, they might think they have escaped their problems, but the reality is that the abuse will most likely continue until the victim gets help.

Peer Pressure

"Let's get totally wasted," said Larry, Saman-tha's friend. Samantha didn't say anything,

but she didn't want to drink tonight. She was planning to audition at school for West Side Story *in the morning, and she wanted to try out for the lead.*

Everyone else wanted to drink. When Larry offered Samantha a beer, she wanted to say no, but Juan, the guy she liked, was sitting right next to her. So she took the beer, hoping Juan would think she was cool.

After drinking the beer, Samantha poured herself a glass of orange juice. Juan was watching, so she added a shot of vodka to it. Feeling nervous around Juan, Samantha guzzled her drink. It made her feel calm and less nervous. She thought she'd stop drinking then, but what if Juan thought she was a loser for not wanting to drink anymore? Things seemed to be going so well, she wasn't sure she should risk it.

Peer pressure reveals the insecurities you may have about being one of the gang. You're at a point in your life when you're trying to figure out who you are. It's only normal that you want to fit in. When friends or peers drink to be cool, you feel that you have to drink, too—otherwise you're not cool and you don't fit in. This simply isn't true. The next chapter suggests ways to say no to your friends and still feel good about yourself.

CHAPTER 4

How to Say No Without Saying No

*O*n Friday night, Stephanie was at a keg party with her best friend, Angela. Stephanie talked with Angela before they arrived. Stephanie said she had decided she didn't want to drink anymore. Angela said she'd back her up, since she didn't want to either. They were going to stick together and be a team.

They knew that the pressure to drink would be tough on them. They decided then and there that they would work toward a goal that would make it easier to stay sober. Since they both loved to run, they decided that they would start training for the next marathon. It felt more secure to have a plan.

When Stephanie and Angela arrived at the party, their friends were already drinking. When someone tried to pass them each a drink, *they both said, "No, thanks." They gave their* *reason. Their friends were surprised. Some tried to tease them and said, "Just one won't kill you." But Stephanie told them, "You can't drink if you're training—and we're training."*

Taking Action

Stand Up for Yourself

It's tough trying to stand up to peer pressure. But when you do, you may actually find that people respect you more for it. Once you establish that you don't drink, you may find that people won't continue to pressure you.

Do Some Prep Work

Planning ahead always helps. If you know you don't want to drink, think about how you're going to deal with the pressure. Plan out what you're going to say before you find yourself standing by the keg with what seems like the entire school watching you.

Say the Right Thing

Stand in front of the mirror and practice what you're going to say to get your drinking buddies off your back. Ask an older sibling or friend what he or she said or did in that same situation. Just about everyone has been in this situation at some point.

Breaking Myths

MYTH: Wine coolers are more like soft drinks than alcoholic beverages.

FACT: Many wine coolers may taste like soda or fruit punch, but they actually have as much or even more alcohol than a twelve-ounce can of beer.

MYTH: Beer isn't as bad for you as wine or hard liquor, such as vodka or whiskey.

FACT: Not true. The amount of alcohol in a twelve-ounce can of beer is the same as a five-ounce glass of wine or a one-and-a-half-ounce shot of liquor.

MYTH: If you drink too much, the worst that will happen is you'll end up with a nasty hangover the next morning.

FACT: Drinking excessive amounts of alcohol is potentially deadly. CSAP says that 2.6 million U.S. teenagers don't know that a person can die from an overdose of alcohol.

MYTH: I don't have an alcohol problem if I only drink on weekends.

FACT: You don't have to drink every day to be a problem drinker. "Episodic drinkers might only drink twice a year," says Nancy Chase, public health adviser for CSAP.

Thinking Long-term

Do you find yourself in high-pressure drinking situations even though you've tried hard to avoid them? Do you find it difficult to stay sober around your friends? The following are some suggestions on how to stay sober in these types of situations.

Talk with a Friend

Be honest. If your friend hasn't been as supportive of your sobriety efforts as he or she could be, talk about it. Be careful not to lay blame. Just be clear that you wish to avoid alcohol and you need help. Together, you might be able to find ways to make it easier to stay sober.

Your friend might also be able to take a more active role in high-pressure situations. For instance, if other friends are giving you a hard time, he or she could intervene on your behalf. Others may be more likely to leave you alone if they see you have support from another person.

Avoid Alcohol as a Group

Talk with your friends. You might think they love to pound beers, but they might do it because they think you do. As a group, you might decide to go to the movies instead of a house party on Friday night.

Respect yourself—and your interests. Maybe your friends drink because they think *you* like to drink. If you'd rather see a movie than go to a keg party, speak up and do it!

Work Toward a Larger Goal

Get involved in an alcohol-free activity that interests you. Working toward a larger goal will help you endure peer pressure. When you get more involved in other activities, you have much more to look forward to than getting bombed on a Friday night.

Take a Stand Against Alcohol

Many teens are becoming aware of the dangers of alcohol and are forming groups like Students Against Destructive Decisions (SADD), formerly Students Against Drunk Driving. In these organizations, you can take action and help to educate your peers.

Take the Keys

If your friend has been drinking, make sure he or she doesn't drive. If possible, take the car keys. No matter what, don't get into the car with him or her behind the wheel.

What Should You Do First?

If you suspect that your friend has been drinking, talk to him or her. You don't want to make judgments or criticize your friend for being drunk. "Try to get on the same side and then suggest another alternative for both of you," says Bill Cullinane, president of SADD. Say, "I don't think you're drunk, but we've had a few beers and if the cops stop us, they'll take away our licenses."

What If Your Friend Gets Violent?

Try to get help from someone nearby. Keep calm and try to stall the situation as much as possible. But be careful. Physical violence will make the situation worse for you, your friend, and whoever else might get involved.

Can You Avoid a Scene?

Yes. Talk to your friend in private, away from the crowd. An intimate talk might sway your friend to hand over the keys. But in front of a crowd, there's more pressure to rebel or act like it doesn't matter.

40 | **What If You Were Depending on Your Friend for a Ride?**

Call another friend, your parents, a brother or sister, or a cab. (You should always carry money for cab fare whenever you go out.) You might think your parents will be upset, but they'd rather pick you up than have you take a ride with a drunk driver.

You can also plan ahead with your parents for this kind of emergency. To make it easier to ask for your parents' help in front of your friends, Cullinane suggests devising a code phrase with your parents. When you call from a party and say, "There's no way I'm going to clean out the attic," your parents will know to pick you up at a certain location.

Get Buzzed on Life

The key to happiness? You've heard it before: You don't need to drink or do drugs to get high on life. Experts say that anyone can achieve happiness and success.

Daily Meditations

Spend time with yourself. Write in a journal or go for a long walk. This will help you think about what is happening in your life and give you a chance to sort things out. Make a daily list of three great things in your life—appreciate them! Visit the library and check out books of daily meditations. These offer insights on life and may suggest short-term goals that will benefit your long-term plans.

Twelve Step Programs

Thousands of teens are recovering from alcohol problems with the help of Alcoholics Anonymous and its Twelve Step program. If you feel that alcohol is taking over your life, you can find guidance from this program.

The road to recovery isn't an easy one. The Twelve Step program has a strong base in spirituality. It breaks the goal of recovery into steps, each building on the other. For those who follow this program, it's important to get a firm grasp on one step before moving to the next. This program is an ongoing, lifelong strategy for recovery.

In the Twelve Step program, alcoholics admit that their addiction has taken control of their lives, and they look to a higher power for help in recovery. Along the way, they explore the mistakes they have made and resolve to admit faults and to improve themselves. They also come to recognize the positive qualities in themselves. They think about those people they have hurt

You may find that when you are sober, you have more time and energy to do the things you really love to do.

and try to repair those relationships. **43** Finally, they use what they have learned from the program in everything they do and spread their knowledge to other alcoholics.

Do What You Love
Some teens say they drink because they are bored. Think about all those things you love to do, such as listening to music, painting, taking photographs, or playing sports. If you don't have any particular hobbies, now is the time to explore new interests!

Get involved with different activities. Join a club, take lessons in something you like to do, or intern at a hospital, newspaper, radio station, or veterinary clinic.

Set Goals
Be realistic. Most likely your grades have suffered because of your drinking. So don't expect yourself to go immediately from being a D student to an A student. But if you work hard, the As may not be too far off in your future.

Break your larger goal into smaller goals. Congratulate yourself when you achieve them.

Spend Time with Your Folks
Try to keep your parents in the loop. If they know what's going on, they are less likely to nag you about everything. Confide in

44 them. You might think they don't get it, but believe it or not, they might surprise you and offer some decent advice. And if you've set new goals, they might get excited and help you achieve them.

If talking with your parents always seems to end in arguments, write them a letter explaining how you feel. This will give them a chance to find out what you're trying to say before jumping to quick conclusions. If, however, you have an abusive parent, you need to get help. You can call hotline numbers for help, and you can remain anonymous (see the Where to Go for Help section at the back of this book).

CHAPTER 5

If You Can't Stop Drinking

Lately Anne was spending less time with her friend Kisha and more time with the "cool" party crowd. Kisha felt left out. She didn't like the way they drank all the time. Every time Anne was with that crowd, she was always drunk. At the party Friday night, Anne was slurring her words.

Kisha remembered how Anne used to stay after school in the library to do her homework, but now Anne was blowing off her work all the time. When she failed her last science test, she said, "I don't care. It's just a stupid test, anyway."

Kisha finally spoke to Anne. She said she thought Anne had a drinking problem and should get help. Anne got really angry.

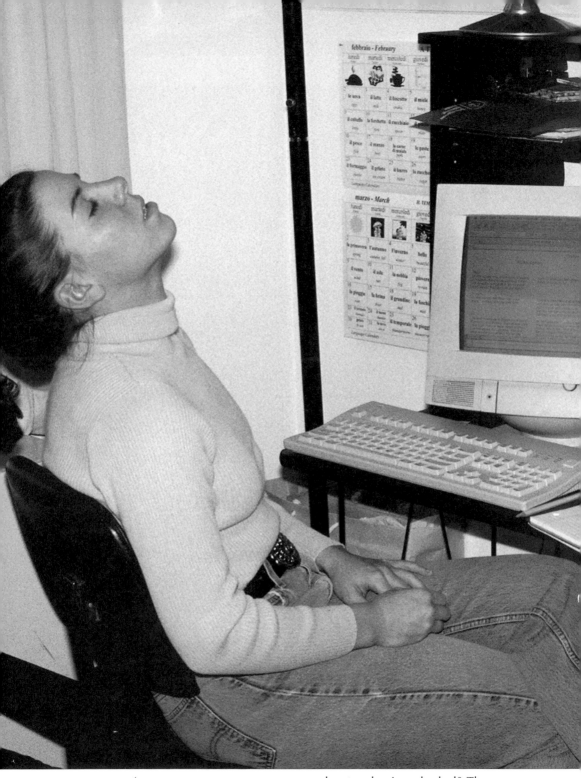

Are you—or someone you care about—abusing alcohol? There are several warning signs, including loss of interest in school-work, athletics, and/or physical appearance.

"I don't drink any more than anyone else does," Anne said. "You're just jealous that other people want me as their friend and not you."

Kisha was stunned. Her best friend seemed like a stranger. Maybe there was nothing she could do.

Warning Signs

Do you suspect that someone you know abuses alcohol? Watch for these symptoms. One or more of these symptoms may be signs of alcohol abuse.

- Mood swings and unpredictable behavior
- Loss of old friends in favor of new party friends
- Defensiveness about the right to drink
- Loss of interest in physical appearance
- Loss of interest in schoolwork, athletics, family, job, or other interests
- Lower grades
- Excessive fatigue and sleeping problems
- Loss of appetite
- Personality changes when drunk
- Tendency to endanger the lives of self or others when drunk

48 | *Do You Have a Problem?*

Ask yourself the following questions:

- Do you really look forward to drinking?
- Do you drink more than you intend to?
- Do you drink to ease such feelings as sadness or loneliness?
- Do you rely on the feeling you get from alcohol as a means of escape?
- Do you think a party's not a party without alcohol?
- Do you need to have alcohol to have a good time?
- Is drinking a significant part of your life?
- Do you drink alone?
- Do you need a drink before you go out to a party?

If you answered yes to one or more of these questions, you might have a drinking problem. Seek the help of friends, parents, siblings, and professionals who are trained to help people with drinking problems.

The First Step to Recovery

If you have a drinking problem, don't feel alone—you're not. The U.S. Department of Health and Human Services reports more

More than one-third of all high-school seniors drink five or more drinks in a row at least once in a two-week period.

than one-third of all high-school seniors consume five or more drinks in a row at least once in a two-week period.

You can recover. But first, you need to deal with the fact that you have a problem. It's a problem that won't go away—and will probably only get worse—unless you get help. If you can't talk to your parents, speak with an adult you trust. You can also get involved with a self-help group where other teens deal with the same problems.

If Your Friend Is the One Who Is Hooked

The best thing you can do is let your alcoholic friend know that you care, but remind him or her to seek professional help. Your

49

50 friend might deny that he or she has a problem and may even get angry. However, your friend will probably thank you later for caring enough to speak up. Here are some tips about how to approach a friend who has a drinking problem.

Talk When Your Friend Is Sober

When a person is under the influence of alcohol, he or she may not be able to think clearly. Confronting someone who is drunk might make the situation worse. Talk with your friend later when he or she is sober.

Express Concern in a Nonjudgmental Way

Say, "I'm worried about your drinking." Your friend might then get angry at you or deny the problem. Try to trust that your friendship will see you through and that your friend is listening.

Find Information on Alcoholism

You can check out books from your local library on the subject or send away for information from different organizations, such as Alcoholics Anonymous. Learning about the illness can help both you and your addicted friend.

CHAPTER 6

Help Is Out There

*A*ddiction to alcohol is tough to break. You have to want to stop drinking, and you need ongoing support to get well. If you are trying to recover from alcohol abuse or if you have a close friend or relative who is trying to stop drinking, you have a few options for getting help. The right recovery group depends on your situation and what feels right to you. This chapter explores some of your options.

Support Groups

Many recovering alcoholics find support groups particularly helpful because they allow you to meet people who are in similar situations. This might help you not feel so alone, and you may even find yourself feeling stronger emotionally.

51

52 | **Alcoholics Anonymous (AA)**
This support group uses the Twelve Steps as its guiding principles and is made up of recovering alcoholics. Members meet every week. With the help of others in similar situations, members learn how to deal with their alcoholism. Everything that is shared during meetings is confidential. You don't even tell others your full name. Sessions are free.

Al-Anon and Alateen
These support groups help people with friends or family members who have alcohol problems. Alateen is for teens and Al-Anon is for adults. However, if there is not an Alateen group in your area, an Al-Anon group may be helpful.

One of the first things you'll learn in Alateen is that you are not responsible for someone else's drinking habits. You will also learn that you are not the only person dealing with an addicted loved one. Like AA, Alateen enforces confidentiality and the sessions are free.

Professional Therapy
AA, Al-Anon, and Alateen groups are not professional counseling groups. They allow people to work out some of their problems with other people who are in similar situations. In professional therapy, you will be

working out your problems with a trained |
professional.

Professional therapy will help you deal with issues and learn about what caused you or your friend or family member to start drinking. You may be interested in getting involved in both individual and family therapy.

Individual Therapy

In individual therapy, you meet privately with a psychologist, psychiatrist, or social worker. You learn how to cope with problems instead of avoiding them and turning to alcohol for escape. This type of therapy gives you a chance to talk confidentially one-on-one with someone about your situation. You discuss how to deal with your feelings. Some coping techniques include:

Reframing. "Teens tend to see things in black and white," says Jane Cranston, therapist on staff at the Alcoholism Council of New York. She uses reframing as a method to help her patients see things from a different perspective. For example, you might say, "A glass is half empty." To reframe that, you'd say, "The glass is half full." This helps you to recognize that there are different ways of viewing any situation.

Exercise can offer a natural feel-good high.

Feelings chart. This technique helps teens to develop a feelings vocabulary. The chart might include twenty-five different emotions. "Many teens say, 'I'm bored' or 'I'm frustrated' when they really mean they're angry or sad or anxious," says Cranston. "[A feelings vocabulary] is important because it makes it easier for them to express themselves and give other people a better idea of what's really going on."

Exercise. Thirty minutes or an hour of aerobic activity, such as basketball or running, or another form of exercise you enjoy helps to relieve tension. "It also helps with body image and provides a feeling of accomplishment," says Cranston.

Talk it out. Cranston says it's crucial to find |
someone you feel comfortable with so that
you can talk out your problems. It can be
a friend, parent, sibling, counselor, teacher,
or clergy member. You don't need to feel
isolated or alone.

Family Therapy

This form of therapy involves every family
member. It can help members understand
what role they play in the alcoholic family
and how they can make positive changes to
aid in recovery. This allows the family to
cope with—and overcome—the disease
together. Family therapy can help you learn
coping techniques such as:

Feelings diaries. Each family member keeps
a feelings diary for a week. By writing
things down, you won't mistake or confuse
feelings with thoughts. For example, just
because you feel like drinking doesn't mean
you have to do it. A feelings diary helps the
therapist to gauge what's going on with
each person in the family during the week.

Realizing roles. People play certain roles in
every family. Who is the hero? Who is the
scapegoat, or the one who gets blamed for
problems all the time? The therapist will
help you determine what role you and

other family members play and why. Participants can then decide how they can change their behaviors.

Time and space negotiation. This concept calls for everyone in a family to have personal time and space. Parents and teens learn to negotiate deals. The result of each deal is a compromise: If you promise to do something the parent wants, then the parent will do or not do something, depending on your wishes. For example, if you promise to clean your room once a week, your parents may promise to let you use the car every Friday night.

Setting goals. This means that parents and teens say what they want. A realistic goal is chosen and written down on paper. If the teen gets the B+ that his or her parents hoped for, then he or she should be rewarded accordingly (this should be specified on paper as well). Setting goals gets parents and teens to work together.

Many different forms of help are available (see Where to Go for Help). You don't have to deal with problems alone. The first step can be talking to an adult you trust or calling a hotline. As you talk to people, you

may find out some valuable things about $|$
yourself.

You may find that when you are sober, you have more energy for doing the things you love to do and that you are better at them. You may figure out that you are a strong person who can deal with life instead of escaping from it. You may also realize that you are a good friend by supporting your friend through his or her recovery. All it takes to learn these things is a choice to help yourself or a friend stay sober.

Glossary

abuse To use drugs or alcohol in a way that is physically or emotionally harmful.

addiction The state of being physically and/or psychologically dependent on drugs or alcohol.

alcoholic A person who is addicted to alcohol.

alcoholism A disease in which a person is addicted to alcohol.

binge drinker A person who consumes five or more drinks in a row.

cirrhosis Liver damage that can be caused by excessive drinking.

confidential Secret.

confiscate To take away.

denial Refusal to admit a problem.

dependency A physical or psychological need for the effects of drugs or alcohol.

hallucination Hearing, seeing, or feeling things that are not real as a result of drug use.

impotence The inability to keep an
  erection.

revoke To take back.

sober Not under the influence of alcohol.

tolerance When your body needs more
  and more of a drug or alcohol to get
  the same effect.

withdrawal A painful syndrome that
  affects an addict's mind and body
  when he or she stops using drugs or
  alcohol. Symptoms may include aches,
  chills, sweating, hallucinations, nausea,
  and anxiety.

zero-tolerance laws Underage drinking
  laws in thirty-seven states that declare
  that if you are under age twenty-one
  and are caught driving with any
  amount of alcohol in your system, you
  can lose your license for a certain
  period of time.

Where to Go for Help

If you need help or want to learn more about alcohol, alcohol abuse, and alcoholism, you can contact one of the following groups.

Hotlines

Alcohol Treatment Referral Hotline
(800) ALCOHOL

Covenant House Nineline
(800) 999-9999

D.A.R.E.
(800) 223-3273

Organizations

Al-Anon/Alateen Family Group Headquarters, Inc.
World Service Office
1600 Corporate Landing Parkway
Virginia Beach, VA 23454-5617
(757) 563-1600
(800) 356-9996
Web site: http://www.al-anon.alateen.org

Alcoholics Anonymous World Services, Inc.
475 Riverside Drive
New York, NY 10115
(212) 870-3400
Web site:
http://www.alcoholics-anonymous.org

Center for Substance Abuse Prevention
5600 Fishers Lane, #800
Rockwall II Building
Rockville, MD 20857
(800) 729-6686
Web site:
http://www.samhsa.gov

Mothers Against Drunk Driving (MADD)
National Office
511 East John Carpenter Freeway, #700
Irving, TX 75062-6233
(800) 438-6233
Web site:
http://www.madd.org

National Association for Children of Alcoholics
11426 Rockville Pike, Suite 100
Rockville, MD 20852
(301) 468-0985
(888) 554-2627
Web site:
    http://www.health.
    org/nacoa

National Clearinghouse for Alcohol and Drug Information
P.O. Box 2345
Rockville, MD 20847
(800) 729-6686
Web site:
    http://www.health.org

National Council on Alcoholism and Drug Dependence
12 West 21st Street
New York, NY 10010
(212) 206-6770
(800) NCA-CALL
Web site:
    http://www.ncadd.org

SADD (Students Against Destructive Decisions)
P.O. Box 800
Marlboro, MA 01752
(508) 481-3568
Web site: http://www.
    nat-sadd.org

In Canada

Alcoholics Anonymous
Greater Toronto Area Intergroup
234 Eglinton Avenue East, Suite 202
Toronto, ON M4P 1K5
(416) 487-5591

Clean and Sober Addiction Consultants
18-1110 Henderson Highway
Winnipeg, MB R2G 1L1
(204) 334-7595

Mothers Against Drunk Driving (MADD)
National Office
6507C Mississauga Road
Mississauga, ON L5N 1A6
(905) 813-6233
Web site:
    http://www.madd.ca

For Further Reading

Coleman, Sally, and Nancy Hull-Mast. *Our Best Days*. Center City, MN: Hazelden, 1990.

Coleman, William L. *What You Should Know About a Parent Who Drinks Too Much*. Minneapolis: Augsburg Fortress Publishers, 1992.

Kahn, Timothy J. *Pathways: A Guided Workbook for Youth Beginning Treatment*. Rev. ed. Brandon, VT: Safer Society Press, 1996.

Landau, Elaine. *Teenage Drinking*. Springfield, NJ: Enslow Publishers, 1994.

Plant, Martin, and Moira Plant. *Risk-Takers: Alcohol, Drugs, Sex and Youth*. New York: Routledge, 1992.

Taylor, Barbara. *Everything You Need to Know About Alcohol*. Rev. ed. New York: Rosen Publishing Group, 1996.

Index

64

About the Author
Christina Chiu is a freelance writer in New York City. She was a writer and editor at the Children's Television Workshop and Scholastic, Inc. She also worked on a teen Web site at *Parade* magazine. Currently, she is in the M.F.A. program in creative writing at Columbia University.

Photo Credits
Photos on p. 8 by Ira Fox; p. 26 by AP/Wide World; p. 29 by Archive Photos; All other photos by Ryan Giuliani